When the world becomes a
place where you don't need to
get up and leave the house,
get off the chair to talk
to a friend, or walk down
the street once a day...

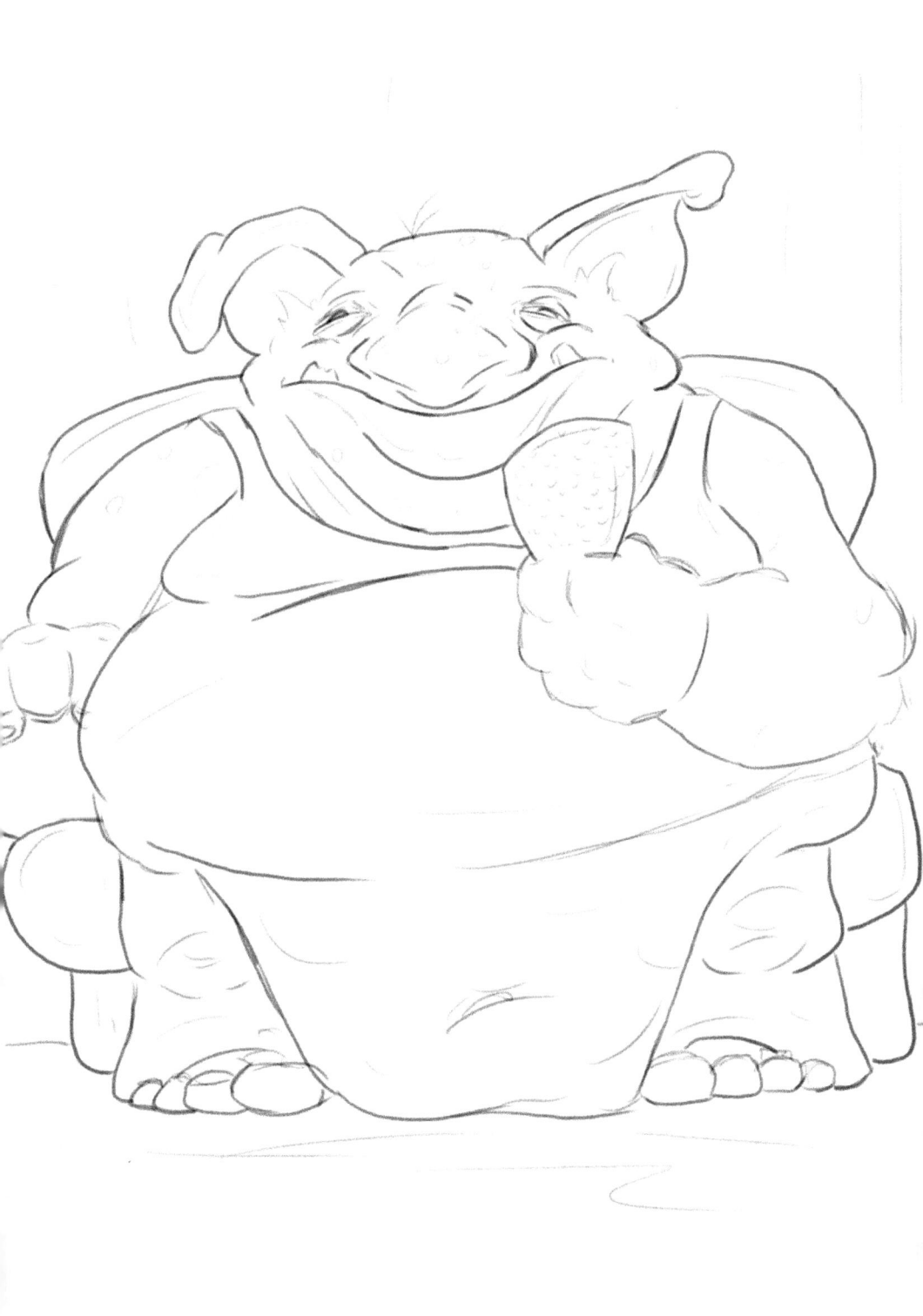

The homeless manster
community is growing...

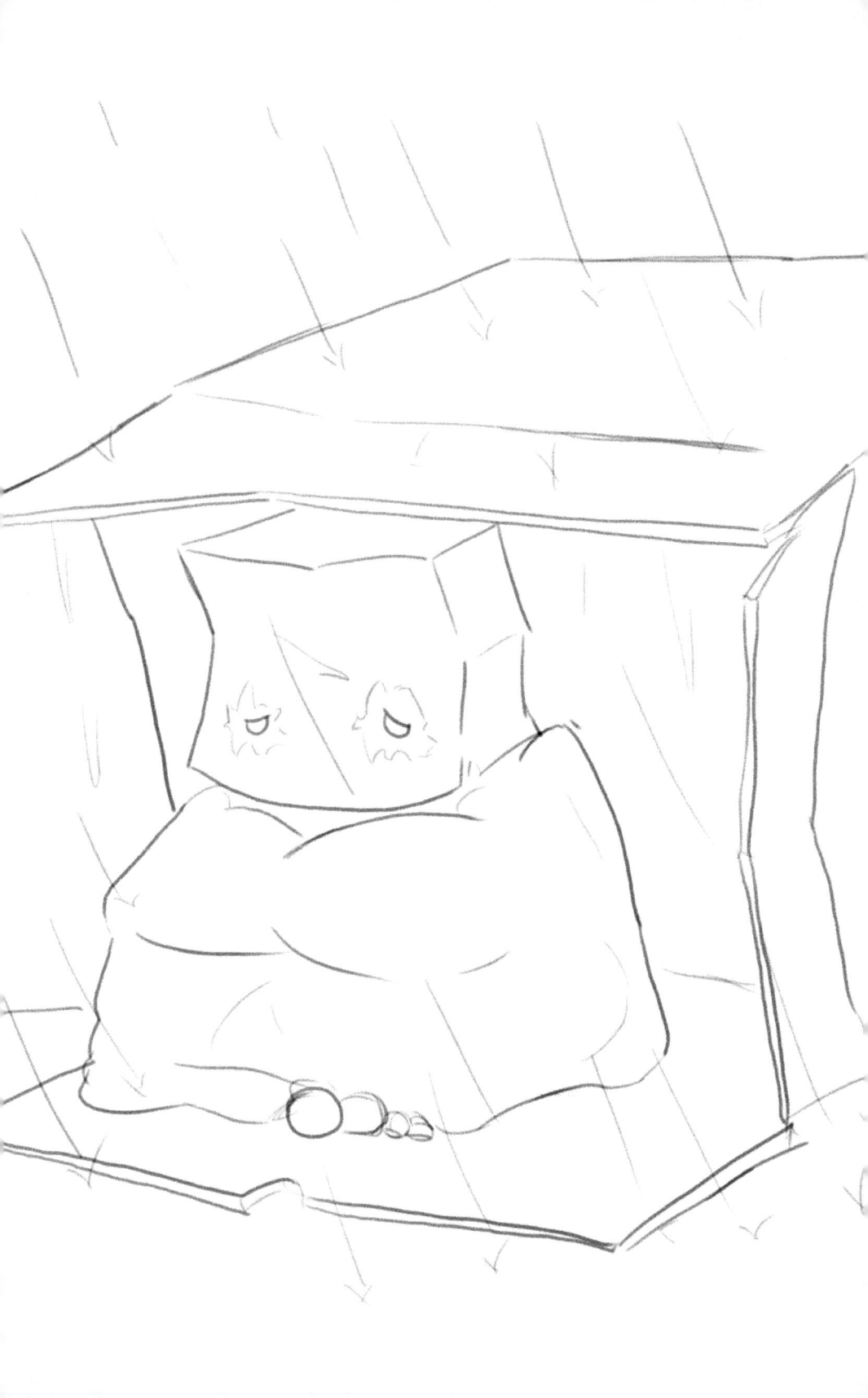

Pills and alcohol can't
solve all your
problems, Andy...

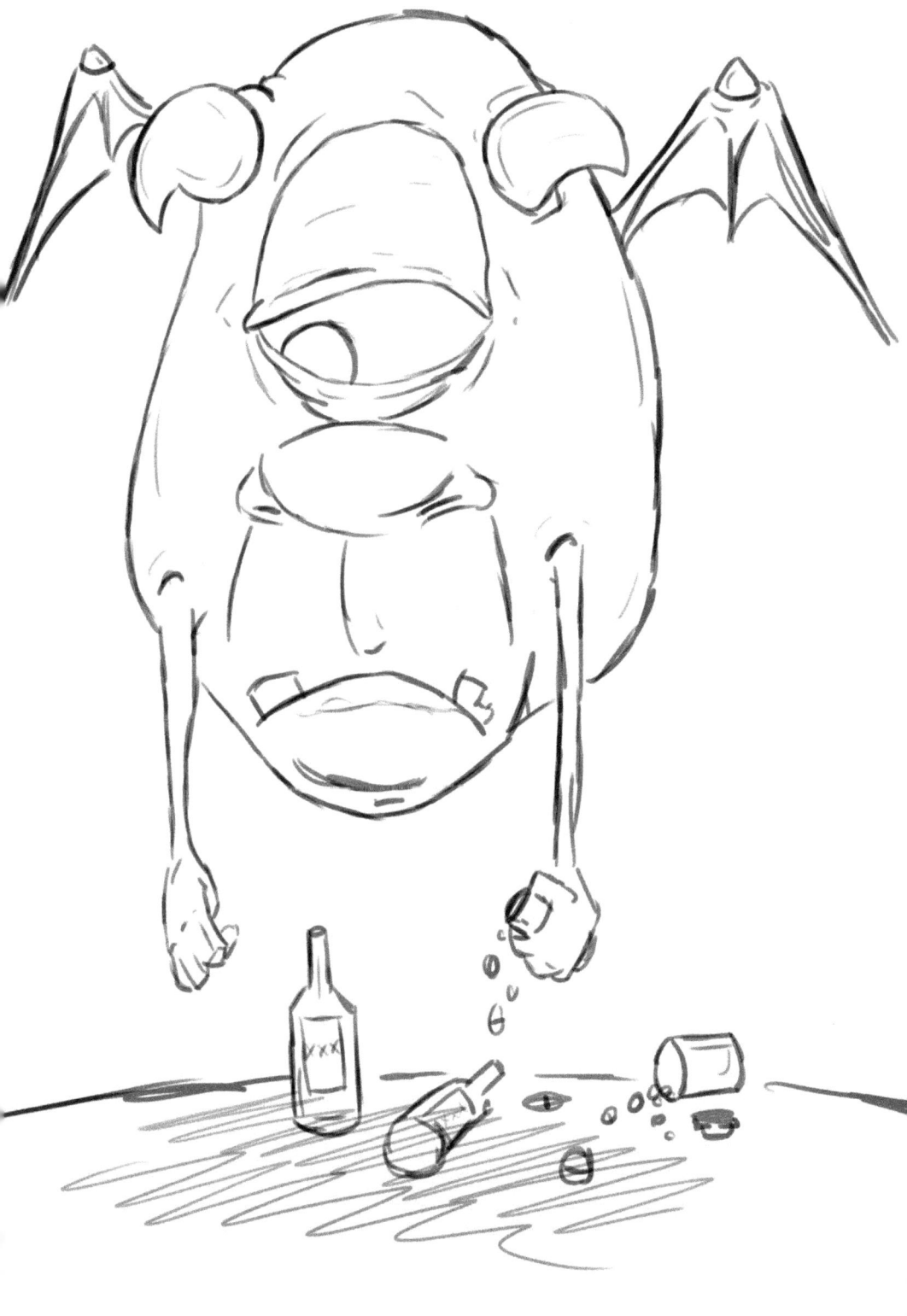

Don won't let us put
trash in his yard.
So it has to go in
Sarah's.

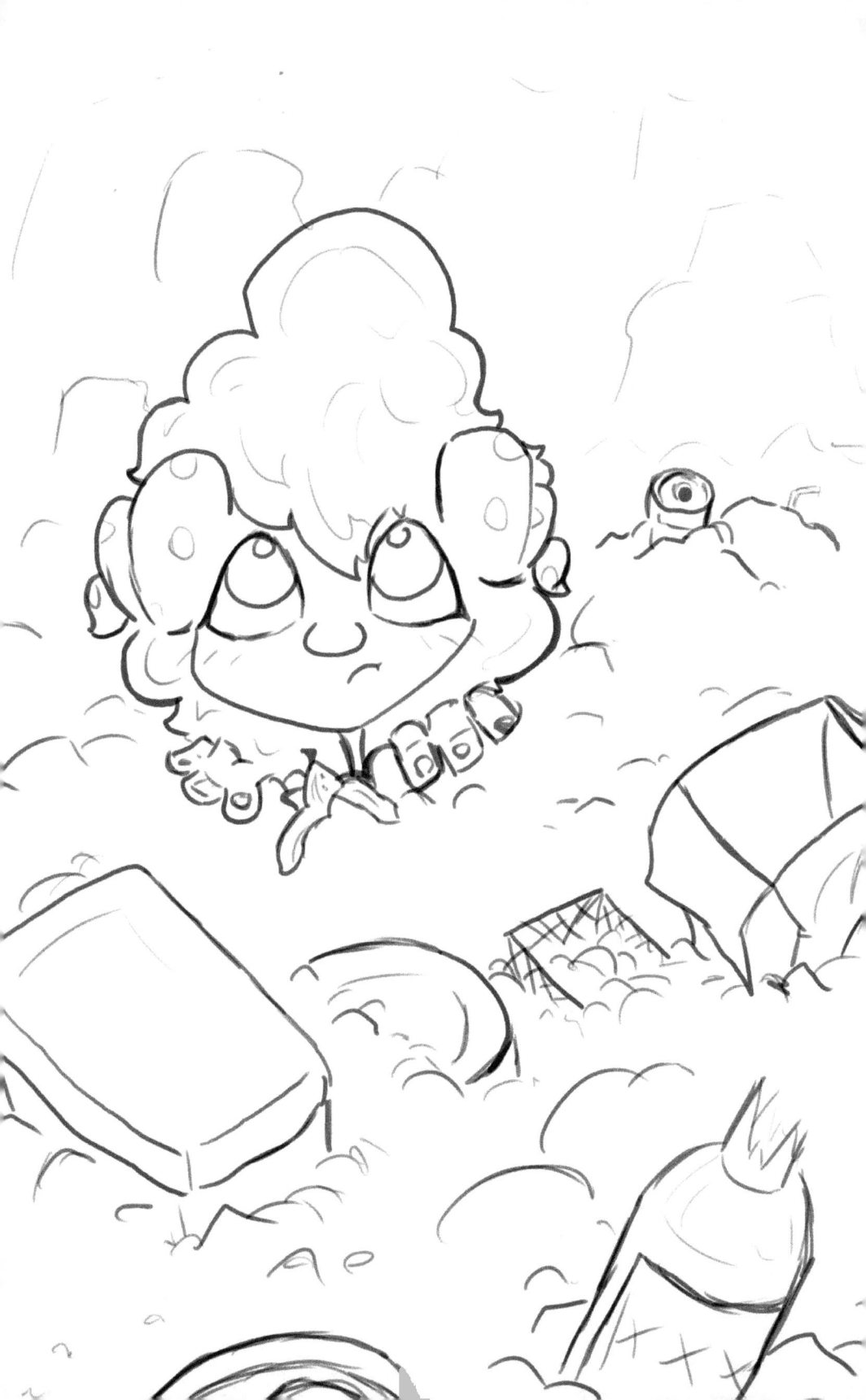

It's June... that's snow... I imagine the smoke stacks have something to do with that.

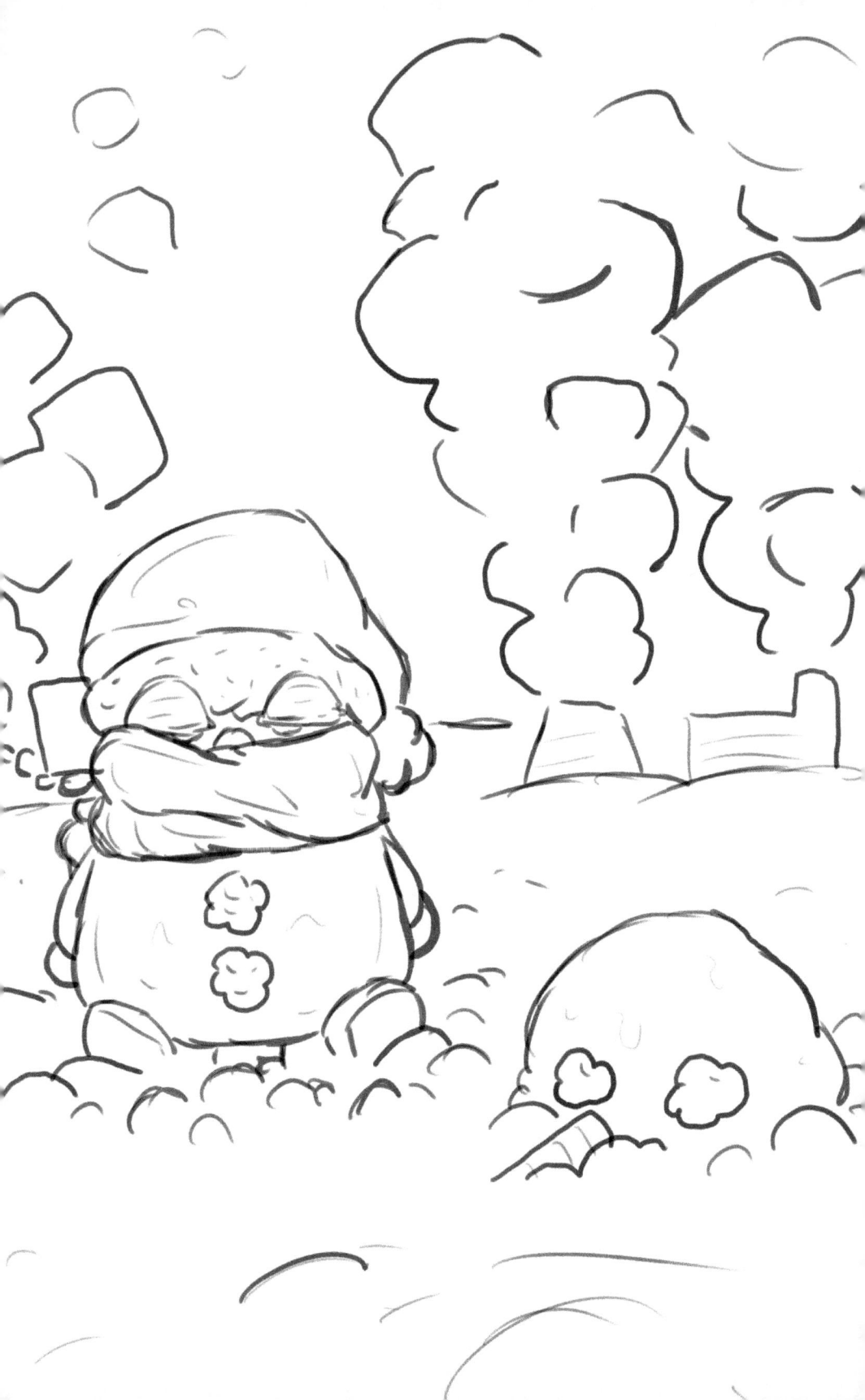

Well... he thought he could move to another country...

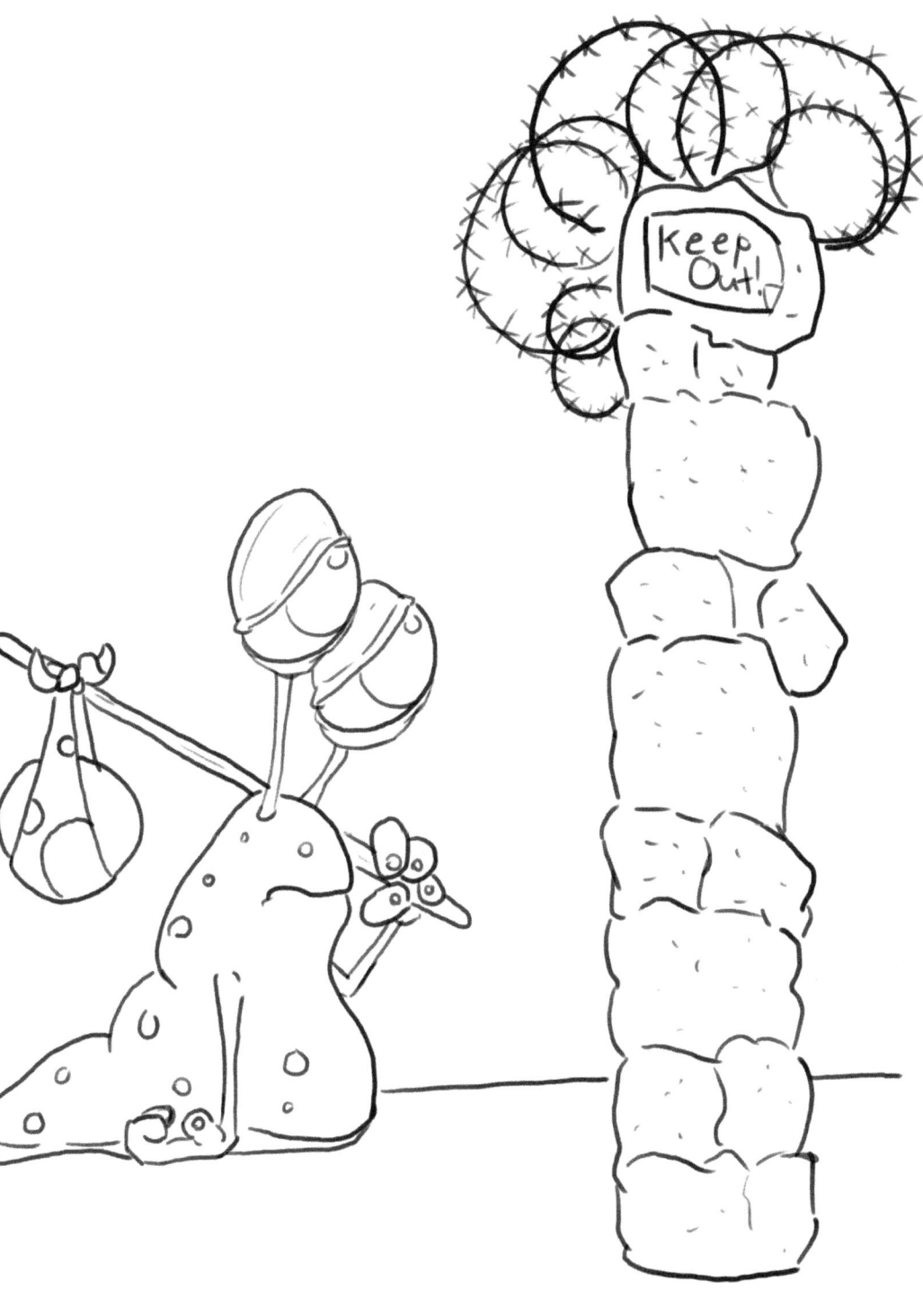

If we lock everyone away, we can hide all of our problems... fixing things sounds like a lot of paperwork.

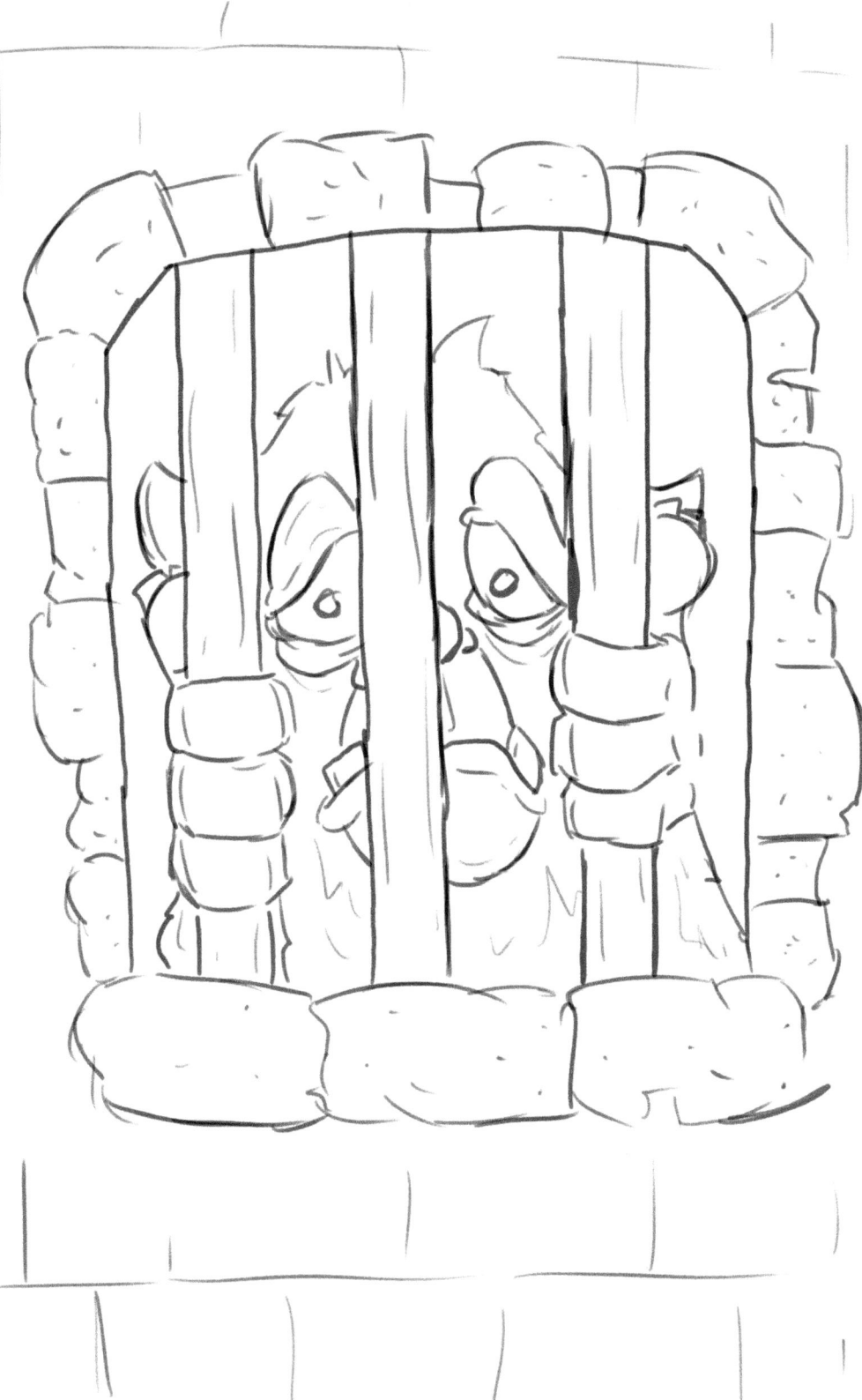

Jeff and Greg have just been married. The town didn't approve.

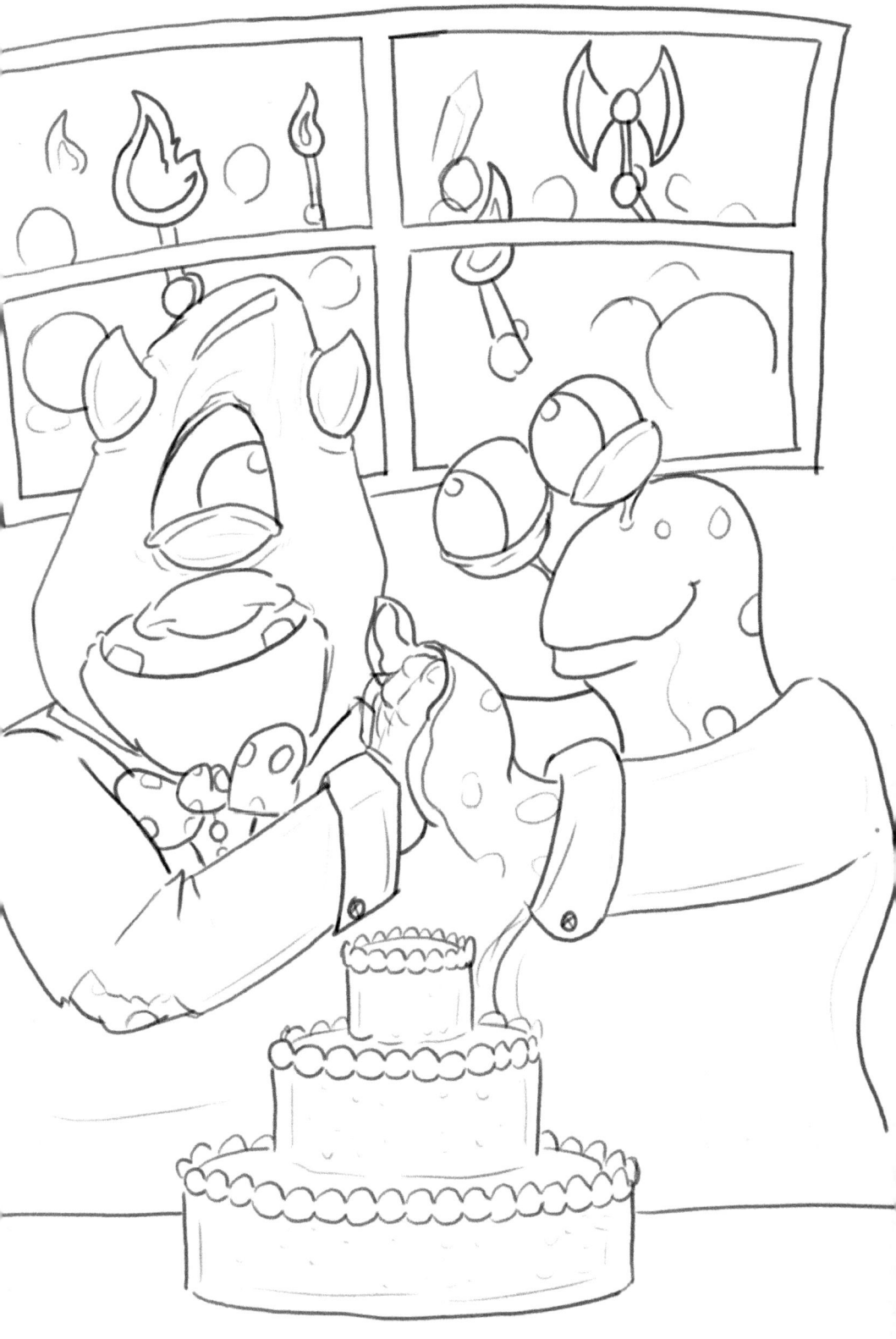

Jamal can't afford to
fix his neck. Doesn't
get healthcare.

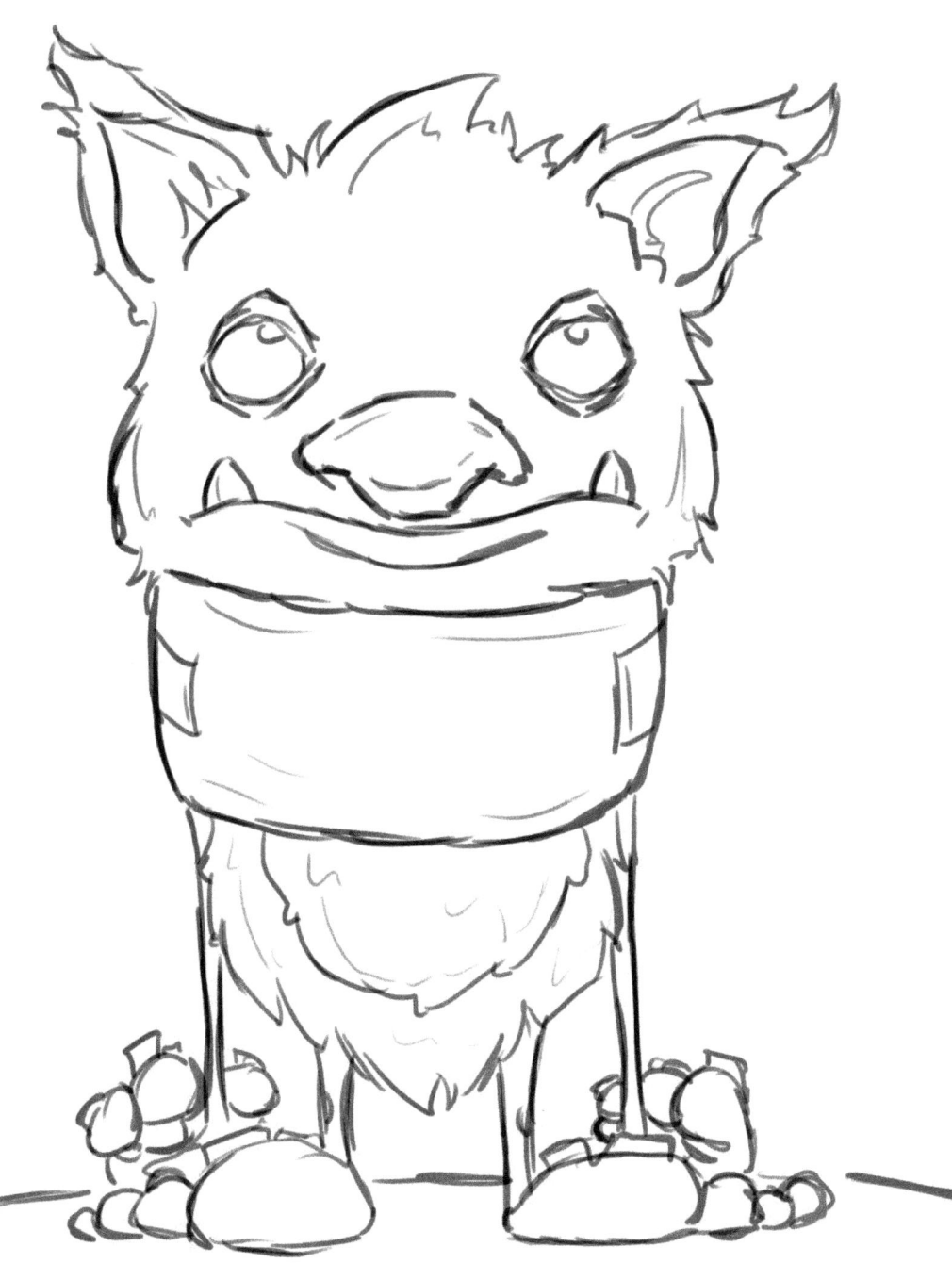

Make sure to congratulate Jim on finishing his 4 years, guys!!!

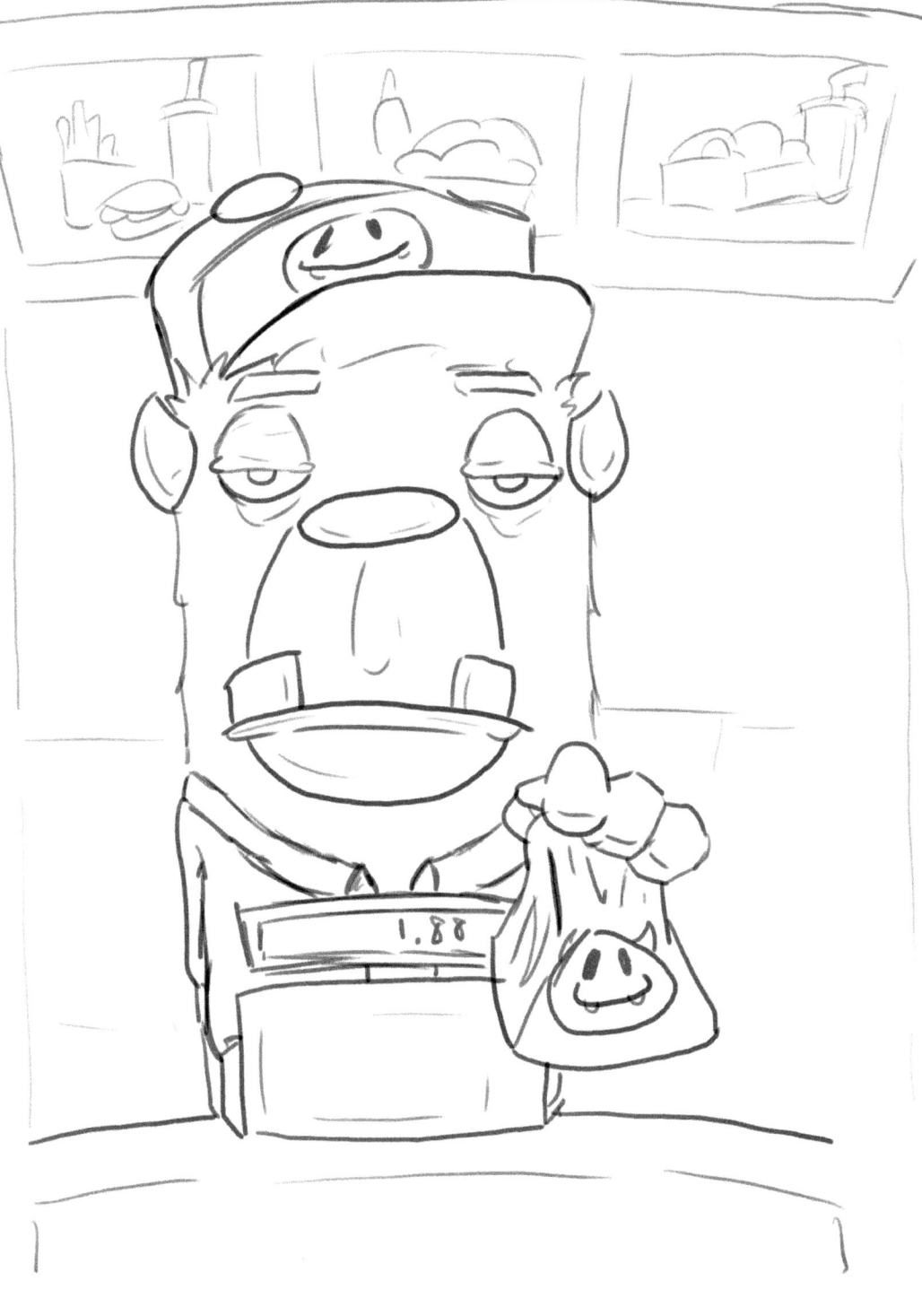

The police officer had

to apologize on T.V.

the next day.

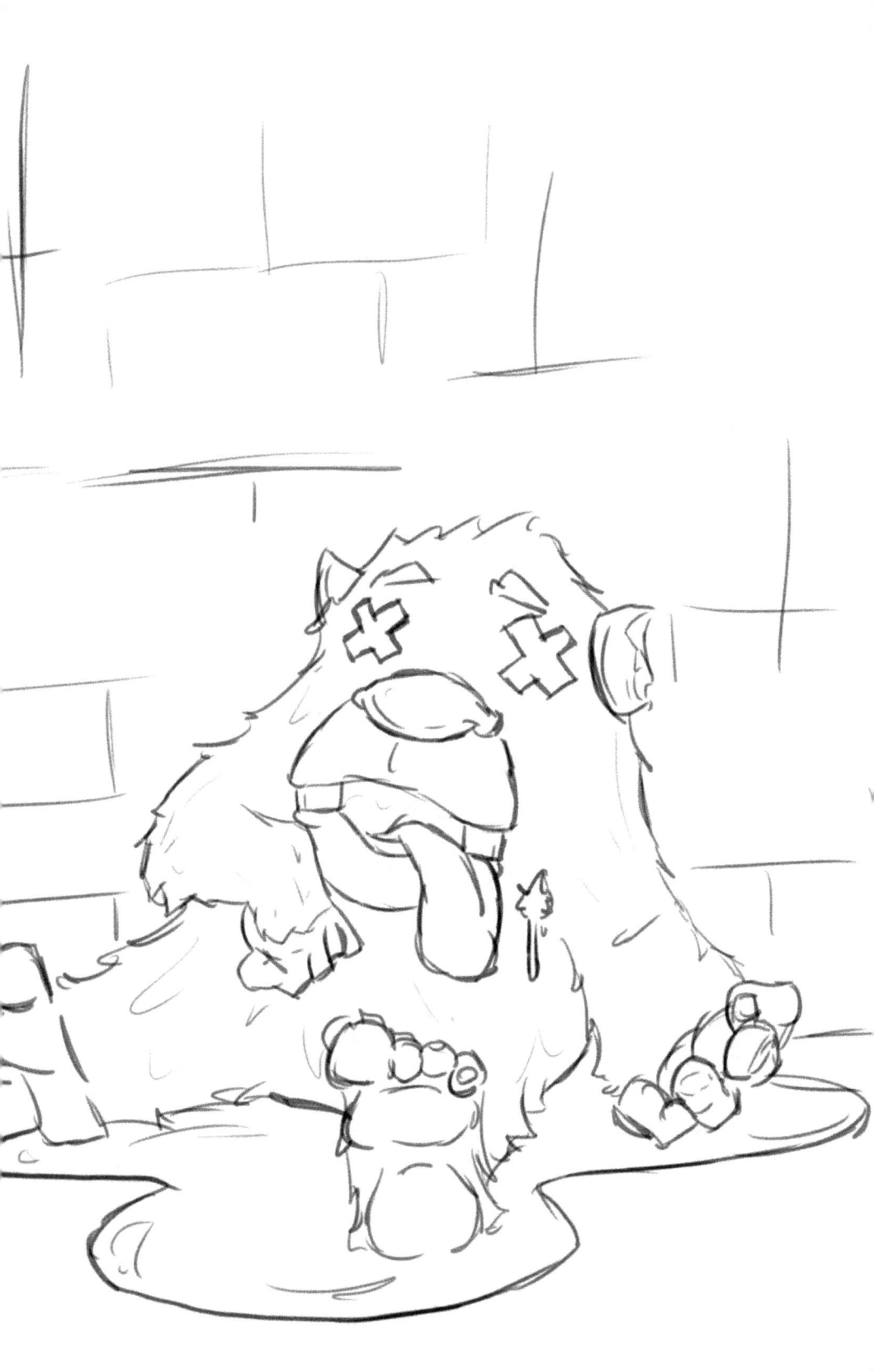

Unfortunately... sometimes it's the loudest monsters who get the attention.

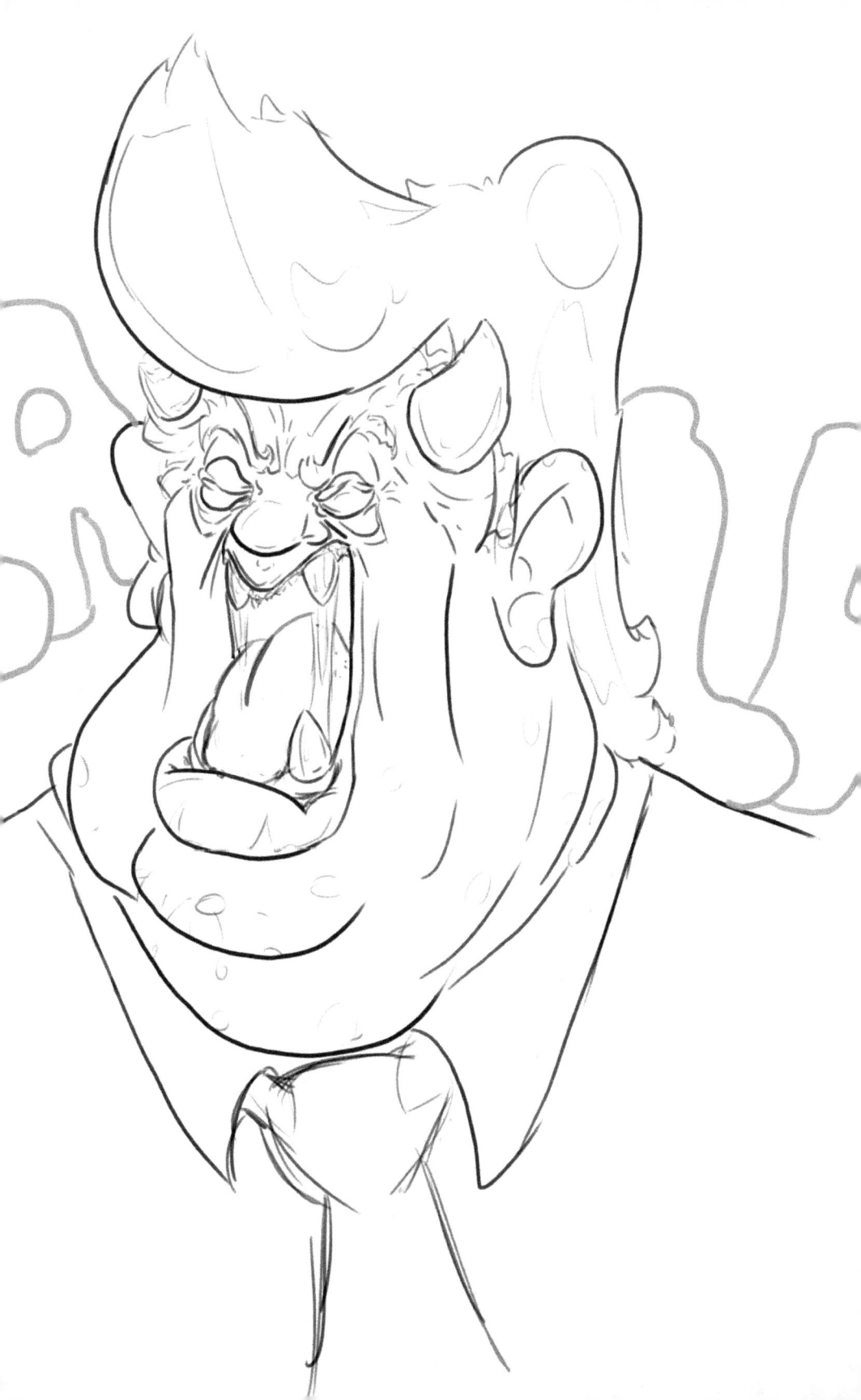

When monsters
can't afford to
take care of their
young...

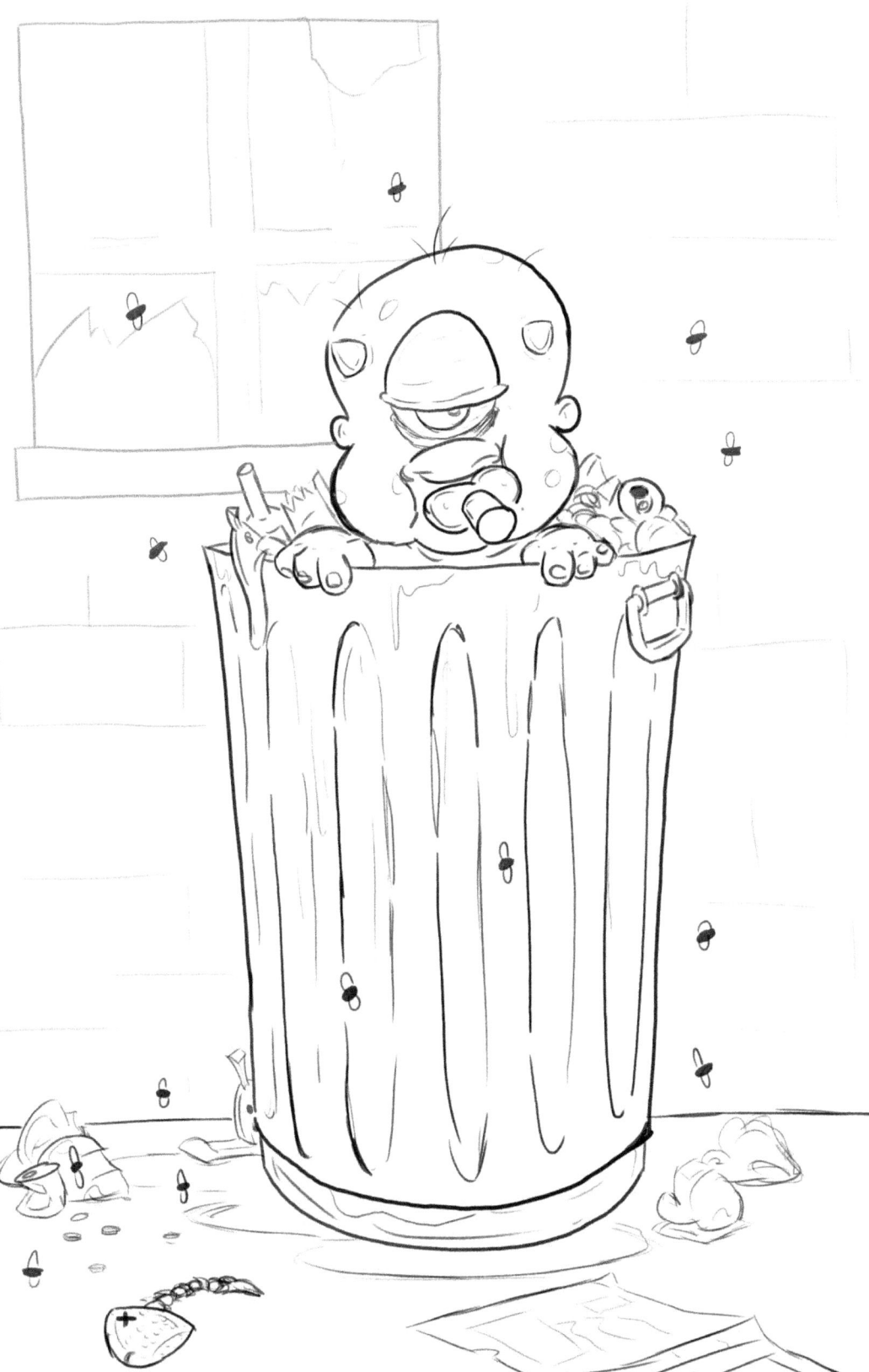

Don owns the food
chain, Monster Munch.
He pays that small guy
a dollar an hour to hold
an ashtray... I don't
know his name.

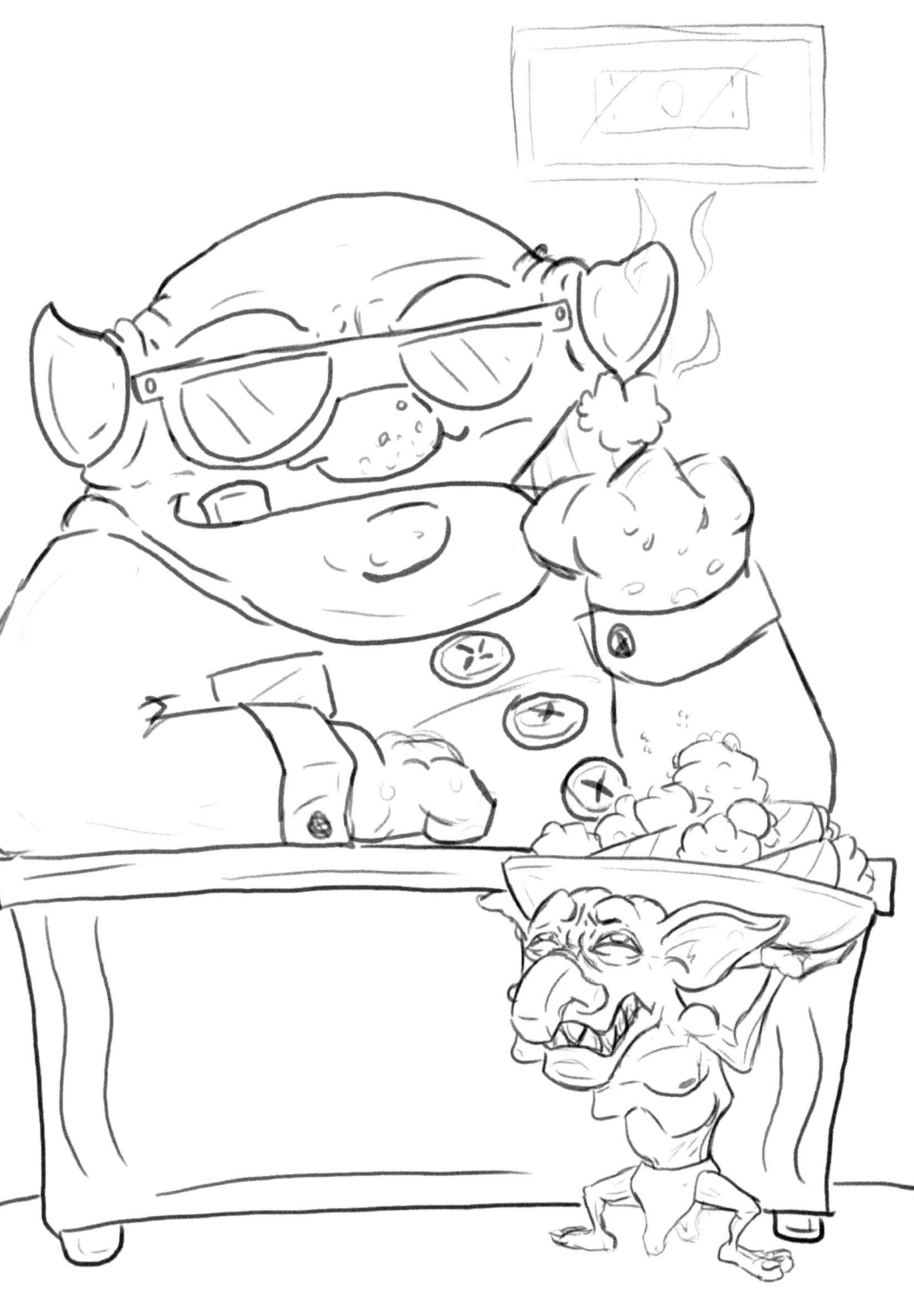

Inside the

Manster Munch

food production

factory...

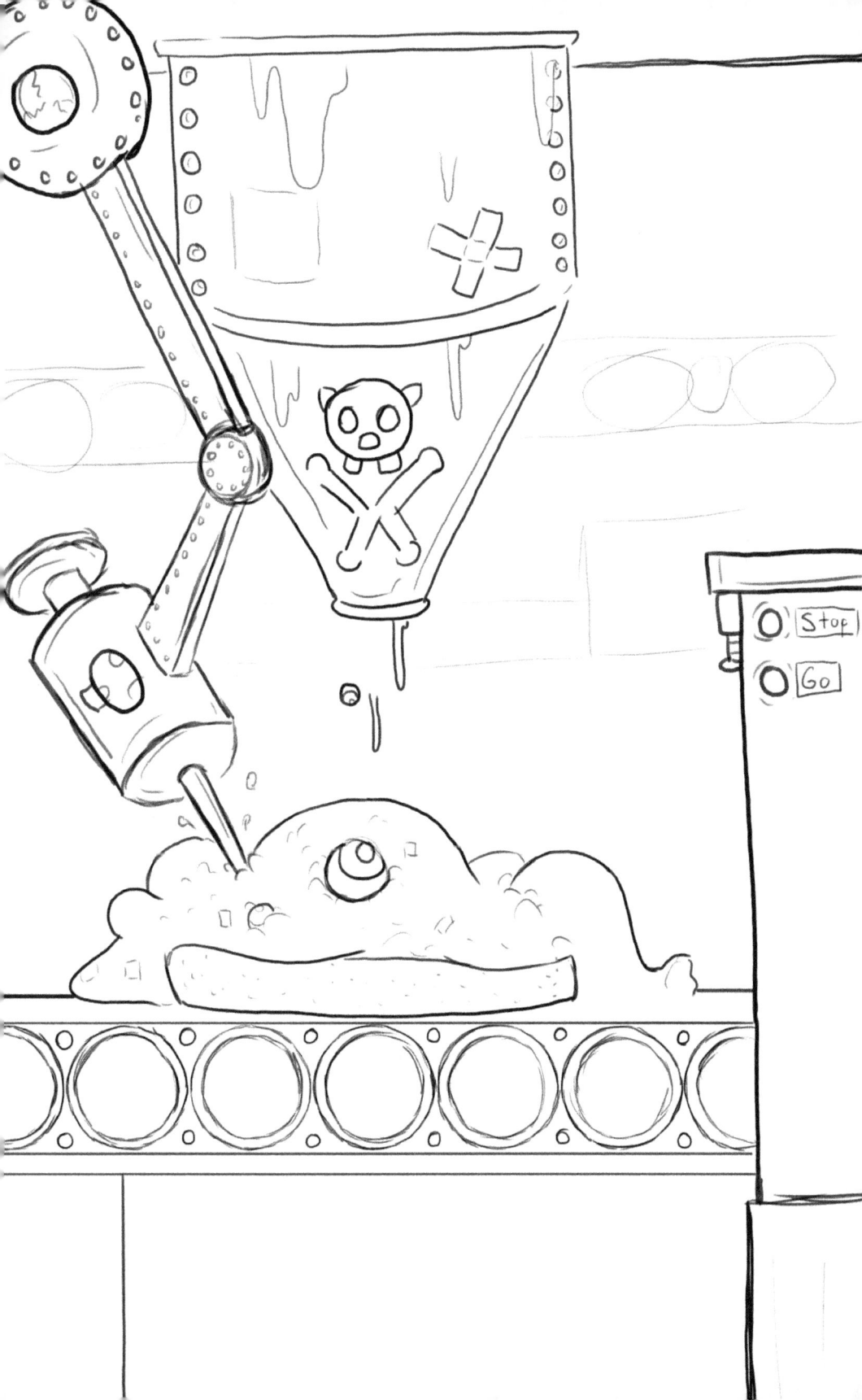

www.ingramcontent.com/pod-product-compliance
Lightning Source LLC
Chambersburg PA
CBHW070429190526
45169CB00003B/1476